The 489th Bomb Group in Suffolk

Who were the 489th & why Norfolk and Suffolk

The 489th Bombardment Group was initially a part of the 95th Combat Wing, of the Second Air Division of the USAAF, which was itself a part of the USAAF Eighth Air Force. After the bomb dump at Metfield was decimated, and the 491st Bomb Group was transferred to North Pickenham, the 489th were integrated into the 20th Bomb Wing.

During the turbulent days of World War II, Norfolk, Suffolk and the wider East Anglia became home to the Mighty Eighth Air Force as it took advantage of the relatively short flight time between the Norfolk/Suffolk coast and mainland Germany to get its war planes to Germany and back in the most advantageous manner. In the latter part of this campaign, Halesworth Airfield became home to the 489th Bomb Group. Made up of the 844th, 845th, 846th and 847th Bombardment Squadrons, Station 365 as Halesworth was known to the American military, was the home to just over 2,900 men who flew and maintained the B24 Liberators of the 489th that operated on an almost daily basis into the German heartland, to harass and damage the Nazi war machine as much and as often as possible.

The 489th were activated in America at Wendover Field in Utah, They flew to England, in loose squadron formations, via the southern route (i.e. Central America, South America, Africa and then Europe) in late April and early May, getting to Halesworth during the first week in May 1944. The 489th's ETO mission was shortest of all 2nd A.D. groups as they were destined to be part of the re-training programme for the B29 Superfortress.

This is how it looked to the men of the 489th recorded on a day to day basis by their own cameras.

Halesworth Aerodrome (Station 365) taken some time after the cessation of WWII.

Originally built as a heavy bomber station Halesworth was used as a fighter station, for almost a year as home for the 56th Fighter Group, before they moved to Boxted in Essex. It was upgraded to a bomber station in April 1944 to accept the 489th Bomb Group in April 1944. The longest runway was North-East / South-West (06/24 – 2000 yards) with the main technical site orientated to the centre left of the photo. The two cross runways were the traditional 1400 yards long and mainly used for landing only, when the wind was not suitable for using the main runway. All runways were the standard 50 yard width, made from concrete and wood chippings. Officially it was home to almost 3,000 airmen.

Halesworth was just over seven miles to the west of the costal town of Southwold, close to the USAAF airfields of Flixton and the ill-fated Metfield of the 491st.

A few months before hostilities ceased, the 489th went back to the U.S.A. and the airfield was returned to the Air Ministry and became home to one of the Navy 762 (Mosquito) squadrons and 798 Squadron who flew Oxfords, before being finally closed in 1946. Eventually, almost two decades later, it was sold and returned to agriculture and became another part of the ever expanding Norfolk based turkey industry.

Although a late arrival to the European Theatre of Operations, (E.T.O.), the 489th had the same mission as the other Groups in the 2nd Air Division; Bomb the enemy as hard as possible and bring the war to an end.

Here the rising cloud of dust, debris and smoke, rising thousands of feet into the air indicate that the new kids on the block could pull their weight on a bombing mission, as the 489th deliver their bomb loads to their allotted destination.

Another day at the office for the 489th…

...and good viz for the day's work.

More 'at work' shots as an enemy aerodrome just out of shot (left), gets the full and undivided attention of the bombardiers of the 489th.

More nose art from the 489th.

The 489th's nose designs were as varied as any 2nd Air Division Bomb Group.

more…

…and more.

But it wasn't all plain sailing for the B24s from Halesworth…

…and some days were always destined to go wrong.

Some days were survivable…

...others plainly were not.

Then there were ones that were spectacular.

The Group Officers 'sweating it out' on the tower, waiting for the first signs of the first plane's return.

Only after the aircrew climbed aboard the truck to de-brief…

…was the thought of this sort of arrival banished for the day.

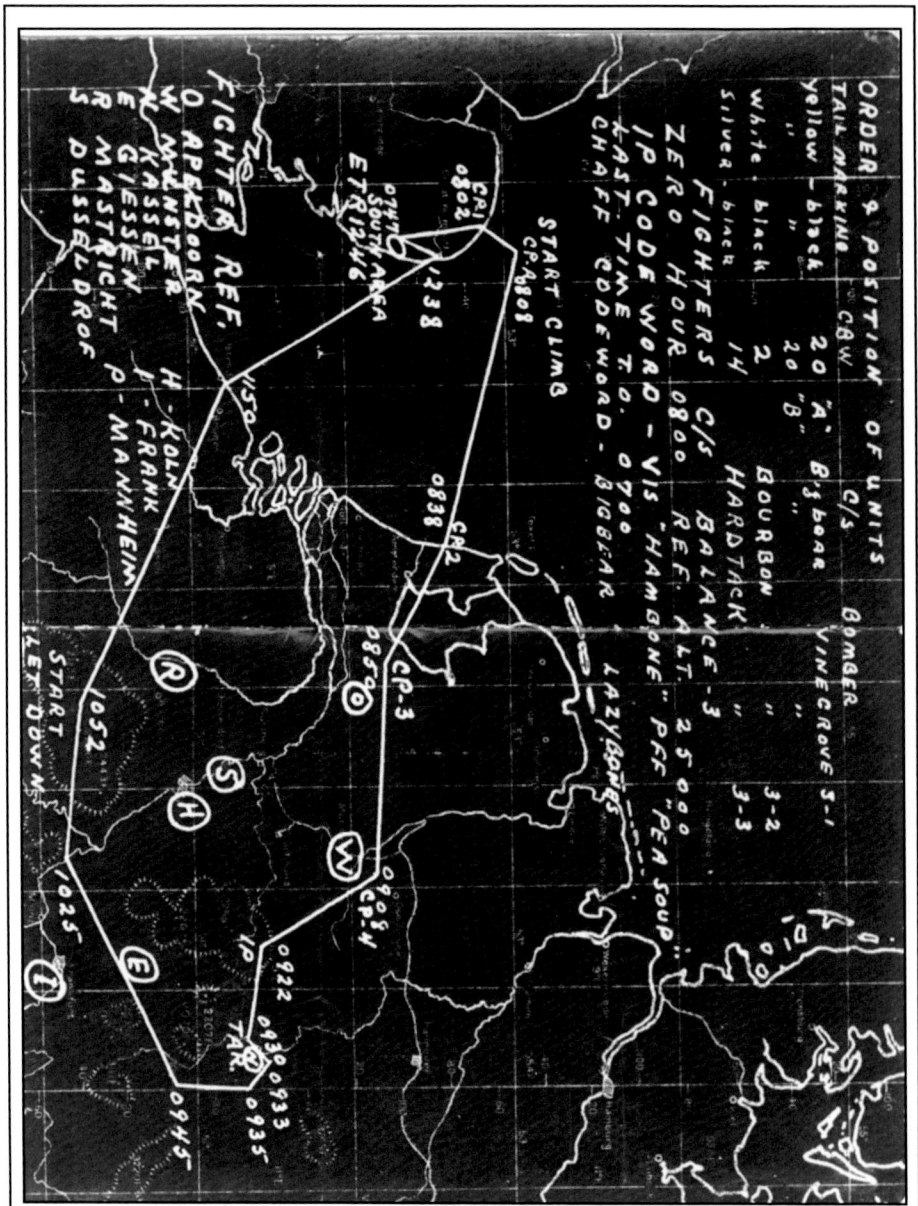

At the briefing, earlier that morning, they gave you your route map for the day.

…and boy had that start been early.

It was not unknown to be in the briefing room several hours before sun-up, and that was after you had all had your breakfast!

Other Gatherings…

100th mission cake!...

…and the Christmas Party.

...the regular crew shot.

…a USAAF standard photograph …

…a must…

...for all crews.

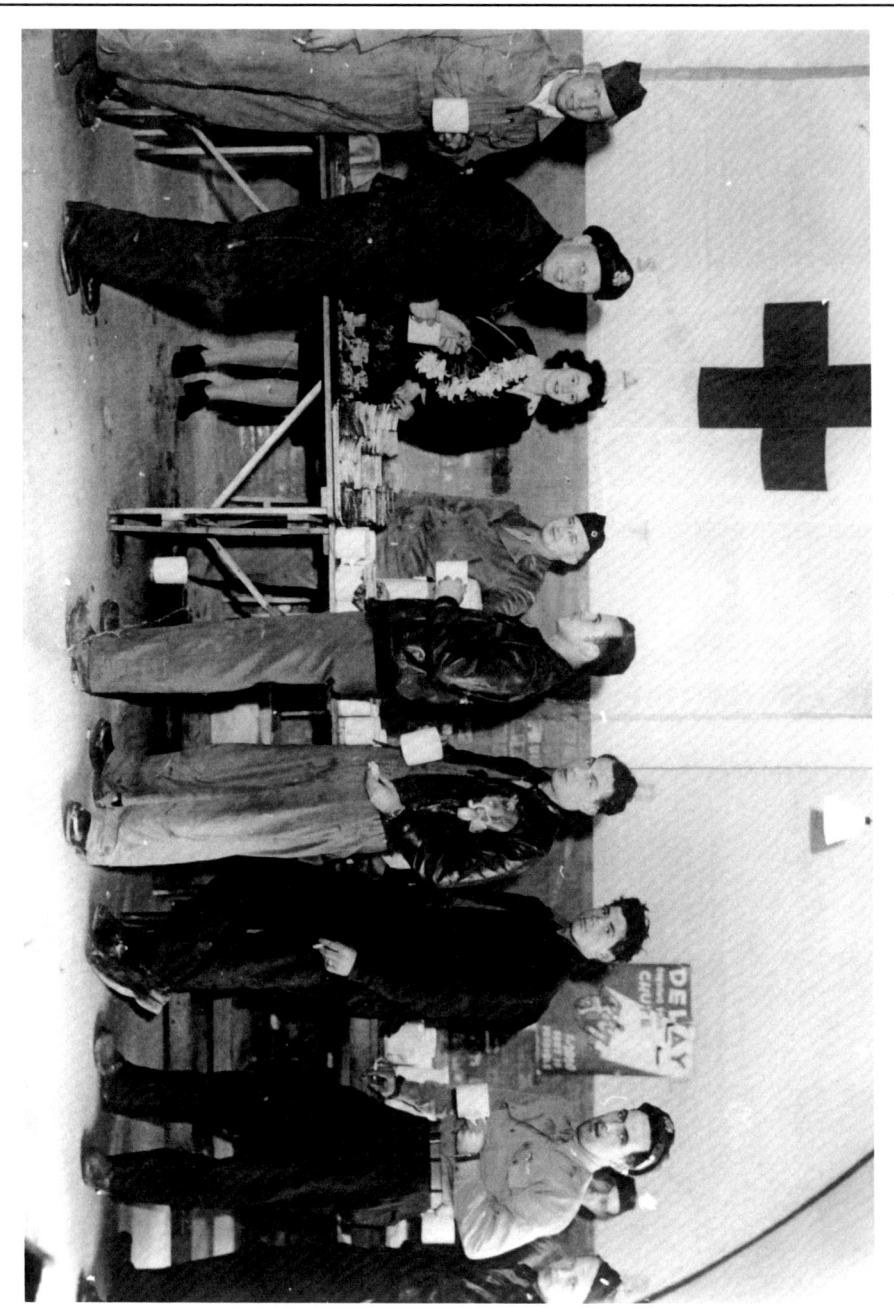

The pre-debrief cup of coffee…

The de-briefing room….

…followed by bed and sleep. Never mind the sun pouring in through the window.

The view from a B24 as you turned into the Halesworth pattern.

Halesworth…

…and Holton.

One of the views across the station…not its best.

Transport; real and imagined, from the ground echelon.

Actual…

…and dreamed of.

One of any USAAF Station's favourite spots.

Relaxing with your buddies…OK then, 'goofing around'.

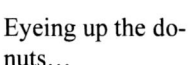

Eyeing up the donuts…

…or watching a ball game…

…or as we said… just 'goofing around'.

Presenting medals was a regular if not routine event. You didn't get to face the enemy on a daily basis without someone going above and beyond the call of duty.

Officers and men of the 489th were indistinguishable when it came to pulling more than their fair share…

…thus the medals regularly went to all ranks.

CONFIDENTIAL

HEADQUARTERS 2D BOMBARDMENT DIVISION
Office of the Commanding General
APO 558

25 August 1944

GENERAL ORDERS)
              :   E X T R A C T
NUMBER 206)

    Under the provisions of Army Regulations 600-45, 22 September 1943 as amended and pursuant to authority contained in Paragraph 2b, Section 1, Circular 56, Hq. ETOUSA, 27 May 1944, and Letter Headquarters Eighth Air Force, 1 June 1944 File No. 200.6, Subject: "Awards and Decorations", the <u>DISTINGUISHED FLYING CROSS</u> is awarded to the following named Officer.

    *   *   *

    <u>HARRY T. WAGNON</u>, O-520509, First Lieutenant, Army Air Forces, United States Army. For extraordinary achievement, while serving as Pilot of a B-24 Group on a mission to Germany, 21 July 1944. Lieutenant Wagnon's aircraft was hit by enemy anti-aircraft fire causing one engine to catch fire, and damage to two other engines, the hydraulic lines, control cables, right landing gear, and fuselage structural members. Extinguishing the fire Lieutenant Wagnon continued with only one engine at full power. Unable to feather the engine that had been on fire, a terrific vibration resulted. Relinquishing the lead, altitude was steadily lost until Lieutenant Wagnon skilfully regained control at 13,000 feet. Exhibiting outstanding flying skill and sound judgment, Lieutenant Wagnon landed his severely damaged aircraft. The determination and superb airmanship displayed by Lieutenant Wagnon in saving his crippled aircraft and crew reflect the highest credit upon himself and the Armed Forces of the United States. Entered military service from Georgia.

    *   *   *

              By Command of Major General KEPNER:

                                                  CHARLES B. WESTOVER
                                                  Colonel   GSV
                                                  Chief of Staff.

OFFICIAL:
    /s/ George L. Paul
    /t/ GEORGE L. PAUL
        Major   AGD
        Adjutant General

A TRUE EXTRACT COPY

L. E. CURRINGTON, JR.
1st Lt., Air Corps,
Intelligence Officer.

If the valour in obtaining honours and the medal itself were the epitome of an G.I.'s militantly service, somehow the 'standard issue' paperwork that went with it seemed somewhat low key.

The crew… and the citation.

The Sharon D

The Sharon D in its home environment.

Both of the Sharon Ds together for possibly the only time.

Sharon D at work and at rest…

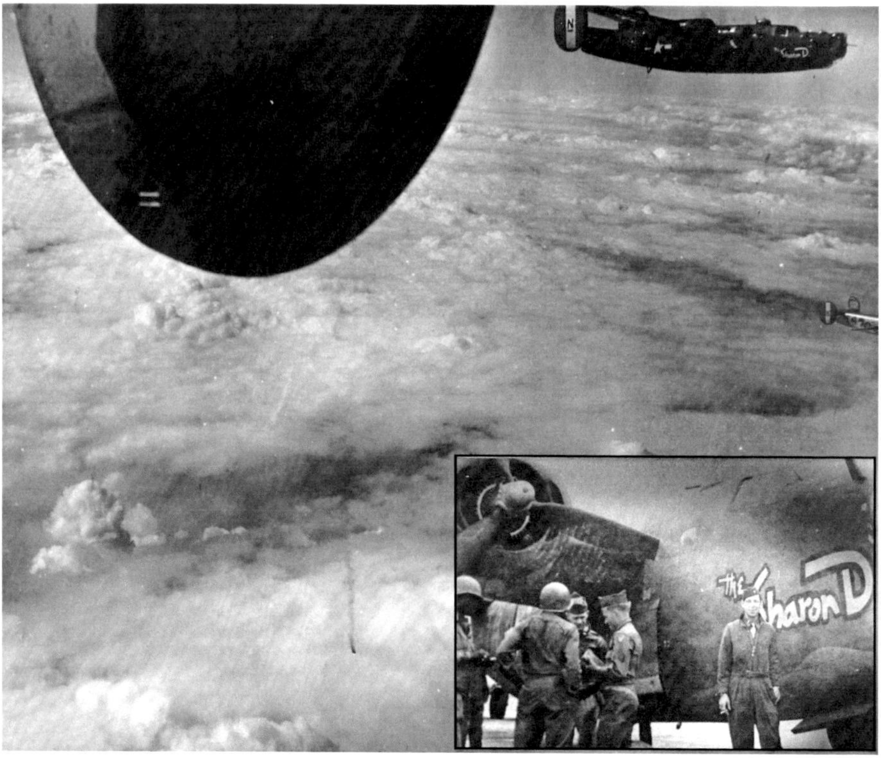

All the 489th pilots including those who flew in the Sharon D spent some time with these guys in the Link Trainer. If you were a pilot you could never be too well trained for your job…

…The Link Trainer, the forerunner to a flight simulator, helped keep all the pilots up to speed with their flying skills.

To produce this effect over enemy installations.

Today's delivery.

The Halesworth delivery team.

The target for today…

The 489th high in the sky above the enemy positions.

Clear sky was good for the bomb aimer…but also for the German fighters.

Great shot to send home !

Parades…

…home made meals…

…or even a picnic outside with the boss.

Hardly a local tourist spot, but the pylons at the local radio station seemed a favourite place for the Halesworth G.Is to have their pictures taken.

As radio was so important, to the war effort, I'm not sure the security section would have been too pleased to know so many shots for the towers were heading homeward to the USA.

Group shots were still pretty favourite…

…as was the local cottage as background.

A convenient local hostelry, complete with it's own bus stop and time-table.

A quaint nearby cottage, greatly used as a backdrop for photos sent home.

The 489th's gunners in full kit.

All dressed up and off to visit the locals.

…and the nearby countryside.

…including the round tower of St Peter's church Holton.

Holton Hall.

Everyday sights around Station 365.

Chow line…

Visitors…

And guys goofing around with things that were designed to go bang!

The strength of the B24 wing being demonstrated at Halesworth.

The waist gunners office.

And a crew shot without the plane…that made it quite a rare photo.

49

The 489th tried nose art on the trucks…

…then progressed to the aircraft. Guys standing by 'their' plane, posing for the shot to send back to the States.

Planes in a bad way often dropped into emergency runways near the coast. Here the 489th's Captain just made it home to the Woodbridge emergency strip and was scrapped where it stood.

The long descent back into Halesworth often started way over occupied Europe.

More good clear targets for these B24s of the 489th.

Some of the 489th nose art on their B24s was rather …different.

Snow White was easily understood, but Lid-on-Lid off and it's question mark, has to be one of the USAAF 8th Air Force's most quirky nose adornments.

Some of the 'my plane' shots at Halesworth were even 'official', as the writing on the bottom edge of the photo shows.

A good healthy dose of 'laddish' humour never went amiss…

…and wasn't confined to the nose of the B24s.

The B29 Boeing Superfortress, was to be the next assignment for many of the aircrew of the 489th. This aircraft was a leviathan of the skies compared to their earlier B24s. Even taxying the plane would have been a rather focussing operation.

There is this stylish memorial to the men of the 489th Bomb Group close to the site of the museum to the 56th Fighter Group, on the site of the old airfield.

There is an excellent Museum to the 489th Bomb Group which is located at Hardwick Airfield, Nr Topcroft village, as part of the Hardwick Museum complex. It is only a short drive from the site of the Halesworth Airfield and well worth a visit.

All photographs from or via the Paddy Cox and Tony North collections.

Cover drawing by Alex Jay.
Alex Jay, 1, Rue de Chateau, Orfveuille, 16140, Ranville. France.
Centre painting by Jim Peters Via Sharon D Vance Kiernan.

For further study, the authors recommend:-
www.489th-bomb-group-museum.org
The Mighty Eighth War Diaries by Roger Freeman. ISBN 1-85409-071-2

Facts and Figures on the 489th

Arrived	1st - 10th May 1944
Departed	29th Nov 1944
Aircraft Used	Consolidated Liberator B24 4 x 1,200 Pratt & Whitney Radial engines 10 man crew Bomb load – 6 tons All up weight – 29 tons Top Speed – 290 MPH Service Ceiling – 28,000 ft Fuel Load – up to 3,516 gallons Range – 2,100 miles
Bomb Group Complement	95th Combat Wing(H)/ 20th Combat Wing(H) 489th Bombardment Group (H) Headquarters 844th Bombardment Squadron (H) 845th Bombardment Squadron (H) 846th Bombardment Squadron (H) 847th Bombardment Squadron (H) 474th Sub Depot 1800th Ordnance Company 983rd Military Police Company 2106th Engineer Fire Fighting Platoon 1235th Quartermaster Company 18th Weather Sqn. Detachment 365 867th Chemical Detachment
Missions	104 (2,998 Sorties)
Ordnance dropped	6,951
Losses 1943-1945	Planes – 41 Men – 398